FACEBOOK ADVERTISING

Step by Step Guide on How to Advertise and Market Your Products on Facebook and Get Maximum Profit – Create passive income from your home

© Copyright 2019 - All rights reserved.

The content contained within this book may not be reproduced, duplicated or transmitted without direct written permission from the author or the publisher.

Under no circumstances will any blame or legal responsibility be held against the publisher, or author, for any damages, reparation, or monetary loss due to the information contained within this book. Either directly or indirectly.

Legal Notice:

This book is copyright protected. This book is only for personal use. You cannot amend, distribute, sell, use, quote or paraphrase any part, or the content within this book, without the consent of the author or publisher.

Disclaimer Notice:

Please note the information contained within this document is for educational and entertainment purposes only. All effort has been executed to present accurate, up to date, and reliable, complete information. No warranties of any kind are declared or implied. Readers acknowledge that the author is not engaging in the rendering of legal, financial, medical or professional advice. The content within this book has been derived from various sources. Please consult a licensed professional before attempting any techniques outlined in this book.

By reading this document, the reader agrees that under no circumstances is the author responsible for any losses, direct or indirect, which are incurred as a result of the use of information contained within this document, including, but not limited to, — errors, omissions, or inaccuracies.

Table of Contents

Introduction 5
Chapter 1: How to Use Facebook Advertising 6
   Tips on Setting Up a Successful Ad Campaign 7
Chapter 2: Creating a Facebook Page For Your Business 20
   Setting Up a Facebook Page 20
Chapter 3: Creating Facebook Business Groups 34
   How to Create a Facebook Group 34
Chapter 4: Using the Facebook Business Manager 39
   Why You Should Use Facebook Business Manager 40
Chapter 5: The Facebook Ads Manager 46
   Setting Up a Facebook Ads Manager Account 46
Chapter 6: Facebook Ad Campaigns 61
Chapter 7: Using the Facebook Events Manager 71
   Installing Facebook Pixel Events 71
Chapter 8: Facebook Pixel 83
   Facebook Pixel Functions 83
Chapter 9: Reasons Why You Should Use Facebook Advertising 91
Conclusion 94
Works Cited 95

Introduction

As you most likely know, there aren't many people not on Facebook these days. Facebook is one of the most used websites, and if you aren't using it to advertise your products or services then you're missing out on a lot of money.

Facebook has the potential to provide you with more customers than you would have ever thought you could reach. Not only are you going to be able to reach out to the customers that you already have, but you'll be able to pull more, especially with a business page, a group, or even sponsored ads.

In this book, you're going to learn how you can use Facebook to grab more customers. If you use Facebook to your advantage, you'll be able to drive your business up which will, ultimately, drive your profits up!

Let's get started and teach you how to use Facebook in a way you probably never thought you could before!

Chapter 1: How to Use Facebook Advertising

Each month, Facebook as over 2 billion users that are active. Each of these users fall into specific categories such as students, business owners, parents, and others who are just looking to share things with their friends. Out of each of these categories, there are people who are ready to connect with you. They may not know it yet, but once they learn about your service or product, they will go from possible customer, to customer.

Facebook ads are one of the most effective ways for you to reach out to those that are searching for your service or product . But, you first need to learn how to use Facebook ads, or you're just going to be wasting time and money.

Tips on Setting Up a Successful Ad Campaign

Before you're able to start your ad campaign, you need to look at these tips will help you to make your campaign more successful.

1. Visuals: The most important part of any Facebook ad campaign is going to be the visual element that is placed into the ad. The visual will be what helps you to grab the attention of those that are interested in what you're trying to sell them. By using an appealing visual, your target audience is going to be drawn to your ad, and are more likely to remember you when it comes time to buy what you're selling.

2. Stay relevant: You don't want to create an ad that is irrelevant to the audience. Yes, you are being charged per click, which makes targeting the right audience even more important. will

3. Be congruent: Facebook ad campaigns can fail quickly if you don't promote the message that you want everyone to grab onto. Take for

example, you're offering a free trial of your software, but you forget to send those who click on your ad to the product page where they can get the free trial. Your ad campaign is most likely going to fail. Always make sure that you are correctly setting up your ad. They can see it a million times, but if they can't access it, it does you no good.

4. Provide value: Give people a reason to click on your ad. You're probably going to be going up against some competition in your business niche which is why you're going to need to provide your customers with value. So, offer them a discount to get them to click on your ad. You can even add in some social proof such as "x amount of people have tried our drinks and you can too, with this discount!"

5. CTA: You may be asking what a CTA is. Well, CTA stands for a call to action. Once you have created your amazing eye-catching ad, you'll want to add an action that the prospective buyer can follow. Usually this action will include language that makes them think, if they don't click now, they're going to

miss out.

Setting Up Your Ad on Facebook

While you prepare your ad to run on Facebook, there are 3 things that you'll need to keep it running.

1. Campaign: The first thing you have to think of is what your advertising objective is. In the end, your objective ought to be to increase your business or to send more traffic to your sign-up page. By knowing what your end goal is, you'll be able to create a congruent ad.

2. Ad set: In your ad set you're going to need to define your targeting strategy. This means that you're going to set how much you plan on spending every day, and how long your ad campaign will run. By knowing who you're trying to reach, you'll be able to create a relevant ad.

3. Ad: This is the last step, and it's where you create your visual elements for your ad. Your ad is now going to be relevant and even have a

distinct value proposition that will end up enticing people to click on it. Make sure to use your call to action.

By understanding how Facebook will run your ad, and the process that you'll use, you'll be able to create a strategy to create a successful campaign.

Ad Formats

The type of Ad Format that you use will depend on what your business is, and what you're trying to accomplish with your ad. Facebook provides you with multiple formats that you can use in order to create an effective campaign.

1. Video: Video ads are one of the best ways for you to show off any products you have to offer your client. Videos are able to inspire your customers to click on the play button, which will tell a story, and help you make a deeper connection with your potential clients. Videos can have links in them that will send your customers where you want them to go so that you're able to get them to your website.

a. Video ads can be placed on mobile feeds, desktop feeds, Instagram, and even an audience network.

   b. Most ads will only be able to have up to 90 characters, must be at least 30 seconds long, can only be 4GB, and it can constantly be looped if you want it to be.

2. Images: Images with links that will send your customers to your website or blog. Images will be similar to video ads, but they will be able to be seen in more places. Make sure you're responding to all the comments on your image so that you can boost that image in rankings so that more people can see it.

   a. Image ads can be put on the right column of Facebook on a Desktop, in a mobile news feed, on Instagram, or in audience networks.

   b. Ads can only have 90 characters, 30 characters for the link description, 25 for the images headline, and it's recommended that the image is at least

1200 x 628 pixels.

3. Collections: These sorts of promotions will be short. These ads will be primarily used on mobile devices and can lead to quick buys and easier discoveries.

a. These ads will be on mobile news feeds only.

b. Your collections ad will not be able to use more than 20% test in the image, the headline has to be at least 25 characters, its recommended size is 1200x628, and the image ratio has to be 1.9:1.

4. Canvas: These ads will be interactive with your client and will feature products that Facebook users can play with on their phone. They should be able to tilt their screen or pinch their fingers to zoom in and out, while getting familiar with what you're offering them.

a. Canvas ads should only be on mobile news feeds in order for them to work properly.

b. The recommended size is 1200x628 pixels, the ad copy should be 90 characters, while the headline is only 45 characters.

5. Carousel: Carousel ads will be similar to canvas ads, but they aren't going to have the same number of interactive features. These ads can be used in a variety of placements and can have up to 10 images or videos. These ads will be effective when it comes to ecommerce or the promoting of several posts at once.

a. These ads will be found on the right column of a desktop feed, audience network, Instagram, and even mobile news feeds.

b. The recommended size for a carousel ad is 1080x1080 or even 600x600. The link description should only be 30 characters, the ad copy should be 90 characters. and the headline should only be 45 characters.

6. Slide show: The slide show ads will tell a story with images, sound, and motion. This process is completed inside of Facebook's campaign generator. or you can even upload your own video. These should only be used if you're trying to find an alternative to the video ads.

   a. These ads can be found on Instagram, the right column of a newsfeed on a desktop, audience network, and mobile news feeds.

b. You cannot use more than 20% text in the image. Your ad copy can only be 125 characters, sound is optional but highly recommended, the video length should be 240 min, and the ratio for the video should be 9:16 or 16:9.

7. Lead generation ads: These types of ads will be perfect to collect different types of contact information. Images, videos, or carousels can be used in order to attract users to click on your ad. From there they will be sent a form to provide you with contact information. Facebook ads are most effective when you offer a free download or a coupon.

a. This ad can be used on desktop, Instagram, audience network, and mobile news feed.

b. The website URL and privacy policy will be required. The ad copy will only be 90 characters, the link description will be 30 characters, the headline will be 25 characters, and the recommended image size is 1200x628.

8. Offers: Offer ads will be perfect to generate sales because you'll be giving a discount on your product. You can use images, videos, and carousels for this ad so you're able to reach new people or even your current followers. Anyone who decides to claim your offer should be given a notification before it expires.

    a. The specifications for this ad will be the same as carousel, video, and image.

9. Post engagement: Post engagement ads are where you notice the words, "sponsored" at the top of the ad. You'll usually have the boost option in order to get more engagement towards your business. Whenever you set up these ads, you need to make sure that you're detailing out your target audience.

    a. These ads are found on audience networks, mobile feeds, desktops, and Instagram.

    b. The ad copy will be unlimited for post engagement. The recommended size is

1200x628, headline is 25 characters, and the link description will be 30 characters.

10. Event responses: Event ads should only be used when promoting special events such as seminars. Images or video can be used in order to capture the interest of your customers. You may want to limit the access to the event, so it's important to set the geographical location, and even demographic settings to ensure that you're not wasting money on an ad that will draw in people who are not even going to attend.

    a. These ads will be shown on the right column of desktop feeds and on mobile news feeds.

    b. The recommended size is 1200x628. The ad copy can only be 90 letters, the description for the link can only be 30 characters, the ad's headline can only be 25 letters long, and the image ratio needs to be 1.9:1.

11. Page Likes: Page like ads will send people to

your Facebook page so that you're able to get more people on your page. In the event that you're worried about how much you're spending on your advertising, then you should remember that you want to get the right kind of people to your page so that it's more effective and that way you're finishing money and getting cheap likes.

   a. Page like ads can be on the right column of a desktop feed and on mobile.

   b. The ad copy will be 90 characters, the headline will be 25, the link description will be 30 characters. The recommended image size will be 1200x628 pixels.

The Placement of Your Ad

The last thing that you look at while creating an ad is the placement of on Facebook. Knowing the proper place to put your ad is going to determine how effective it is. A few of the most common spots where you're going to see an ad are in the right column of the feed on a desktop, in your newsfeed on a desktop or on your mobile device, Instagram, and audience network.

1. Right column ads: These are traditional ads that Facebook has to offer and they will appear on the right side of the news feed. Since these ads will be static, they will be ideal for less expensive clicks and are usually going to provide better conversions. In order to make these ads effective, you need to remember to use an attractive ad and an irresistible CTA.

2. Desktop and mobile news feeds: This type of placement will get a lot of traffic when it's created properly. Desktop news feed ads will be placed in a specific spot on the newsfeed for your pre-determined targeted audience. Video ads will capture the most attention but you're going to end up spending a lot of money if your CTA is not strong enough.

3. Audience network: Facebook is an extensive network and you never know where your ads will find themselves. These types of ads will be retargeting ads where Facebook users are able to discover your ads other places besides

Facebook.

4. Instagram: Ever since Facebook took over Instagram, you're able to put your ads on Instagram feeds and stories. Even though the format of the ad will appear the same, the nature of Instagram is going to be different. So, if you're not already using Facebook, you should focus on Facebook at this time and then move onto Instagram once you've seen how well Facebook works for you.

Chapter 2: Creating a Facebook Page For Your Business

A Facebook business page will make it easier for people to discover and communicate with your business online. You already know that Facebook has over two billion active users every month, which means that having a Facebook page that your customers can come to and look at the things that you have to offer, means that you're more likely to grab their attention. Especially when they are able to reach out to you and ask any questions that they may have.

Setting Up a Facebook Page

1. Sign up: You'll go to facebook.com/business and then click on the create a page button, which will be located at the top, right-hand corner of the page. There will be several business type options that you can choose from. After you have decided on your type of business, you're going to be ready to move on

to the next step. However, if your business page falls under multiple categories, then you need to place it under the one that you think is most likely going to bring the most customers your way.

Now that you have clicked on your business type, you'll be presented with a box that will ask you more information such as the name of your business, subcategory, so on and so forth.

At whatever point you're ready, you should click on the start button. Keep in mind that you're going to be agreeing to Facebook's terms and conditions for a business page, so you may want to look at those before you move on.

2. Add pictures: Now you need to upload a profile and cover picture for your page. It's going to be important for you to invoke a good first impression, therefore, you need to choose wisely. Guarantee that the photos that you're picking line up with your brand and will easily identify what your business is.

Your profile picture will be uploaded first. This picture is going to be the first thing seen when your business is searched, and more importantly, when you communicate with clients. It's additionally going to show up on the upper left of your Facebook page.

If you're a major brand, then you're in all probability going to need to utilize your logo since individuals definitely know your identity. If you're a public figure or a celebrity, then using a picture of your face will work perfectly. However, if you're just a local business, then a well shot image if your product, or your bestselling product, will connect to the customer instantly. Your profile picture will appear as a square when it appears on your page. But it will be cropped into a circle when it shows up on your ads and posts, which is why you don't want to place any vital details in the corners. After you have picked out the picture to use, upload the profile picture.

The next step is to pick your cover photo. The best thing to do is pick a photo that will show the soul of your brand. The cover photo is going to need to be 820x312 for a desktop photo, or 640x360 for a mobile photo. The image must be 400 pixels wide and 150 tall.

3. Explore your new page: Now that you have brought your page to life, it's time to start exploring. Facebook is going to offer you a walkthrough of the features that it has to offer. So, unless you already know how to work a Facebook business page, it's a good idea for you to go through the prompts so that you know where everything is. The walkthrough will only take a few seconds.

4. Add a description: Adding a short description will tell people exactly what your business is. The maximum set by Facebook is 155 characters which is why you don't want to be too elaborate here. You'll click on, "add a short description" so that you can share what your business is about so that you're able to draw in customers. A longer description can be added later. Make sure that you click save or else you're going to have to do this part over again.

5. Create your username: Your username is also going to be known as the vanity URL which is going to tell people how you're found on Facebook. Your username will be able to hold at least 50 characters, however, you shouldn't

try and use all of the characters. Make sure that your username is easy to remember, which is why it's recommended that you use some variation of your page's name. Once you click on, "create a username" for your business page, you're going to have the option of setting up your vanity URL. After you have your username set, you'll click on, "create a username." By doing this, a box will pop up with a URL that you can share with others so they can connect with you.

6. Complete the about section: It's enticing to forget details that can be filled in later, but it's vital for you to fill out all of the fields on your about section when you first start your page. Facebook is usually going to be the first place that anyone goes to for data about your business, and that is the reason you need to give them the majority of the data out of the gate. The more information that you can provide your customers, the more likely they are to come back to you when they need something.

It's a good idea for you to list all of the data about your messenger protocol, such as when there will be someone to answer their questions, and how long it takes for someone to answer them.

In an effort to get all of the information to your customers, you'll select the, "about tab" on the left hand side of your Facebook page which will take you to a page that will allow you to fill out any data about your business. Some of the things that your customers may be looking for are, when your business started, business hours, and how you can be contacted.

There is also a screen that will allow you to create a longer description for your page. You'll simply click on edit story on the right side of the page, where you can fill out a more detailed description informing your clients what you have to offer them.

When you want to input your location and hours, you'll need to select the edit page information, located at the top right of the page. Here you'll have the option to enter everything that your customer needs to know so that they can reach you, as well as, find your business location.

7. Create your first post: Before you start adding people to your page, you need to create a post that is going to inform them of what you have to offer them. You'll have the ability to create a specific post, such as creating an offer or creating a poll. The only thing you'll need to do is click on the options part of your status tab so that you're able to see all of your options.

8. Engage your customers: You've brought your page to life and invited people. You can also use Twitter, your website, and other social media that allow you to put your link so that people can follow you. If you're comfortable with it, ask your customers to leave reviews on your Facebook.

Optimizing Your Facebook Page

After you have set up your Facebook page, you now need to learn how to optimize your page, so you meet your marketing goals.

1. Add a call to action button: there will be a million reasons why someone will view a

business page, but you may not have entered all of the data that they may be searching for. A CTA button will take them to your website which will allow them to find any information your Facebook page is missing.

Facebook has a built in CTA button that is going to make it easy for your customers to find exactly what information they need so they can better interact with your business.

Facebook automatically puts a send message button on your page so that they are encouraged to talk to you through your Facebook messenger. However, this can be changed so that your clients are able to learn more about your business, shop your products, download your app, or even book an appointment.

In order to customize your CTA, you should move your mouse so that it hovers over the send button message and then click on the edit button. From here you can decide what kind of button you want to place at the top of your page. Once you're happy with your choice, you're going to click next.

Depending on the button that you pick, you're going to have to put in some extra details and once you get that done, you'll click finish and your CTA button will be live.

2. Add a pinned post: if you're posting important information for your visitors to see then you'll want to place it as a pinned post. A pinned post is going to sit at the top of your page until you decide to take it down. You'll write a normal post and then you'll click on the three dots that appear next to it once you post it. There is going to be an option that allows you to pin it to the top of the page. Once you have pinned a post, you're going to notice that there is a blue thumbtack next to the post showing that it's pinned to the top of the page.

3. Make the most of your tabs: tabs will show up on the left side of the page and will be things such as your about section and your photos. However, if you're ready to, you can enhance your page by adding other tabs so that your customers are able to have a better experience.

Facebook offers tabs such as Tabsite. A site that allows you to build custom business tabs for contests and specific offers you're giving your customers.

If developing is one of your skills, or you're working with a developer, once you reach over 2,000 likes, you'll have the ability to create custom tabs.

4. Like different pages: being that Facebook is an interpersonal organization, it's a smart thought for you to assemble a network for your business as opposed to utilizing it as an expansion of your online presence. One way that you can build up your community is to like other pages that will be similar to your business but are not your direct competitors.

Take for instance, you're running a business in the local mall, you can share the pages of the other shops that are around you; similar to a chamber of commerce except online. If you're working with a virtual business, you're going to have the ability to feature business that are inside of your industry but could provide extra value to your followers without competing directing with what you're selling.

In order to feature another page on your Facebook page, you'll click on the icon under the page's cover photo and then like it as your page. If you're working with more than one business page, choose the page that you want to like the other business page as.

5. Review your settings: your Facebook page will enable you to go into some fine insights regarding who can control the page, where the page can be seen, and the words that are prohibited from the page. You're also able to see how fans are interacting with the page and who has favorited it.

Your settings table should be thought of as the behind the scenes console for each parameter that you'll be able to customize. You should take a few moments to review the page settings to see what is being optimized so that you can customize and manage your page to be just how you want it to be.

The best way to access your settings is by clicking where it says "Settings" at the top, right side of the page. It's vital for you to check your settings regularly because your preferences and requirements will change while your business and social following grows.

6. Learn from your page's insights: when you understand your audience, you're going to

know what content to post that is going to meet their needs. Facebook Page Insights makes it easier for you to gather data about your fans that are interacting with the content that you're sharing on your page.

Insights will provide you with information that is vital to know about how your page is performing overall because it's also going to give you information on your page's demographics and engagement. You're going to want to review the metrics on your posts so that you're able to understand just what is reaching the most people and where you're reaching the most people so that you can better plan what to share on your page in the future.

A standout feature in insights will be the tools that help you to see how many customers are using the CTA button, your phone number, website, or business address.

7. Link your business page to other social platforms: Backlinks is a tool you can use when boosting the credibility of your business. By doing this, you'll improve your rankings when it comes to search engines. All you have

to do is link your brand's page to whatever site you're using. Always include a link at the bottom of your blog posts and encourage others to do the same so that you can share their page or when they mention your business.

8. The blue checkmark: by getting the coveted blue checkmark on Facebook, you're going to be letting your customers know that you're not a knockoff, but the real deal that way that they are confident in their dealings with you. Below, you'll see the steps that you need to follow so that your page can become verified.

   c. Go to the settings page which can be seen at the head of your business page.

   d. From there you'll click on the page verification section.

   e. Now click on the verify this page next click the button that says get started

   f. Here you're going to have the option to get instant verification or go through a detailed verification process.

      i. Instant verification will result in you getting a call on your business phone number and being provided with a verification code.

     ii. A detailed verification will mean that you're going to verify your page with documents which is going to be where you'll upload an official document that shows your business name and address.

a. After your verification has been received, the request goes under review and then you'll either be confirmed or denied. This process can take anywhere from 48 hours to 45 days.

Chapter 3: Creating Facebook Business Groups

Being able to build up an online community is going to be one of the most important steps to make your business grow. It's going to help you get in touch with your key demographic. Building a Facebook page is great because it can help bring new customers to you. But, what about your existing customers? A Facebook group is going to be a great way for you to keep your existing customers in the loop. Not only that, but you'll also will have the ability to convert those that are, "just looking" into customers that are coming back for more every month!

How to Create a Facebook Group

You most likely have already created a Facebook group before. But, just in case you haven't, let's go through the steps on how to create one so that it doesn't seem so intimidating.

1. Enter the URL Facebook.com/groups into your search bar. This is going to take you directly to the set-up page so that you don't have to search through pages to find what you're looking for.

2. Click on the button that says, "create group". This can be found in the top right-hand side of the page. From there you're going to be asked what your groups goal is.

Tip: It's advised that you pick the, "connect and share" button as your goal so that you're able to keep in contact with your members, and provide ongoing support so that they continue to come back for more.

3. Enter your group name. You're going to need to name your group, and while you do that, make sure that you're naming it something that your customers will remember and mentions the name of your business.

4. Invite members to your group! Invite existing customers to your group because they will interact with you, and because you know that they have an interest in your business.

Tip: Try to avoid adding potential customers until you've completely set the group up!

5. Set up the privacy settings. Make sure that you're not putting your group in a setting that you don't want it to be in. Open groups will be open to the public, which means that everyone can see what is posted in the group and who is in the group. Closed groups can be found by anyone on Facebook but the only people who can see what is posted will be members. Secret groups are just that, secret! The only people who can view the group's content or members will be those that have been invited to it.

6. Enter your group's description. Those that already follow your business know what your company is, but why are you creating a Facebook group? Make sure that you put a description that will tell your members exactly what to expect from the group. You'll also need to choose a cover photo for your group, make sure that your cover picture is reflecting your business properly. It's a good idea to create an image that is going to make the group appear inviting while also featuring your brand.

7. Promote your group so that others can join.

    g. One way that you can promote your group is to advertise it in your newsletters and correspondence that you have with your members already.

    h. Post it on your business page that you just created, and pin it to the top of the page so others can always see it.

    i. If you have the budget, use boosts in order to promote your posts about the group.

    j. Invite people who will be interested in your group.

What's Next?

So, now that you have your group up and going and you've gotten some members, what are you going to do next to ensure that your group continues to stay active, and you're able to engage your members?

1. Post regularly: You should post hot industry

topics that your audience will appreciate being made aware of. Never make them feel like they can't ask you questions, because when questions are asked, this is going to guarantee engagement boosts while other users put their answers in the comments.

2. Share something other than your own content: When you share articles and updates that are not about your business, your group is going to see you as authentic and an authoritative source of information.

3. Use Facebook Features: Take advantage of Facebook Live so that your customers can see the real you and know that it's someone that they can trust. This is also a great time to host a Q&A, or provide your group with exclusive insights.

4. Use ads in order to promote your group: Paid ads will be set so that they are suggested for those in your intended demographic. When you attract more members, you're going to have a better chance to widen your fan base.

Chapter 4: Using the Facebook Business Manager

You've set up your Facebook page and your business group so, what are you going to do now? Now you should look into using Facebook's Business Manager. Facebook business manager gives you the following opportunities:

1. Work with a social agency or social media manager that will help by monitoring the quality of what is being done and keep tabs on the work that is being done for you.

2. You'll have the opportunity to have multiple accounts for your business in one place.

3. You can delegate roles and tasks to your team members so that they get done, and not everything is on you.

However, that is not the only thing that you have the ability to do with Facebook's Business Manager. This tool is 100% free and very secure, and keeps you in charge by allowing you to delegate tasks without having to share your personal Facebook with your business page.

In the end, Facebook business manager is going to make managing your business more professional.

Why You Should Use Facebook Business Manager

So, the first thing that is probably going through your head is why should you be using Facebook's Business Manager when you feel that you're delegating tasks and managing your business just fine on your own.

First, Facebook's Business Manager is going to help you gain access to your pages and different ad accounts so that different roles can be established, and tasks can be assigned to those that are working inside of your business. Even if you're a small business right now, you never know when your business will boom causing you to need help, which adds to why you should allow your team members to be able to access your business page to do the tasks that you send to them. Do not fret, as a business owner, you'll still have full control over giving permission and revoking access to people.

On top of this, it's going to allow you to keep your business pages from mixing with your personal pages so that it's a lot less awkward, and you're not accidentally posting something to your page that shouldn't be there.

Let's not forget to mention again, Facebook's Business Manager is free!

Setting Up An Account

Just as setting up your business and page were, setting up an account with the Facebook's Business Manager is easy too! Let's walk through this process together so you can get through it simply and fast.

1. Ensure that you'll be able to confirm your identity with your personal Facebook page. You need to make sure to have at least one business page as well as have an ad account that can be transferred over to business manager.

From there you're going to be able to sign up for Business Manager. Enter business.facebook.com into your search bar and once the page pops up, click on create account. Here you'll need to enter all the details for your business so that everything can be transferred over from your Facebook to your business manager.

Note: It's highly recommended to have a minimum of 2 admins for your business manager account so that the page isn't placed on just one person. This is also going to keep people from locking others out of the page in the event that a conflict arises.

2. Connect your ad account. You'll now need to connect your ad account using the following steps.

    k. Click on the ad accounts on the left-hand side of your screen.

    l. Choose the button that says claim an ad account in the event that you already have one.

    m. However, if you're new to ad accounts you need to create one by choosing the third option on your drop-down menu.

3. Next you'll delegate the roles to employees and assign tasks throughout the account. The page admin is of course going to be at the top of the food chain and is going to be the only one who can assign tasks. From there, the managers will be able to complete the tasks that you give them, but they are not going to have full access to your page.

To be able to add a new manager you'll click settings and then pick the button that says people on the left sidebar before you move on to adding a new person.

Note: You're going to have the ability to add new managers through their business emails, but they will still be required to verify their account through a personal email.

4. Delegate tasks! Now that your managers have been added, you'll be ready to start delegating page tasks. Here's how you can do that.

n. Select pages or ad accounts. The button that you click is going to depend on what kind of task you're assigning.

o. Choose the page or account that you're granting the manager access to.

p. Next, click on, "add people" and select the managers who will be granted access to have the option of completing tasks

Next you'll have the option to assign tasks such as posting, moderating comments, managing ads, and whatever else you need to be done.

Congratulations, you have set up your Facebook Business Manager account! Once you have gone through these four simple steps, you're now ready to master Facebook Business Manager. If you still find that you need help, Facebook Business Manager offers a FAQ that will troubleshoot all of the common issues you may be facing.

Less Stress But More Control

Thanks to this tool, you're no longer going to need to worry about handling every aspect of your business because you'll have the option of handing it over to people who you trust, know what they are doing; or you may hand it over to hired social media help.

Now you'll have more time, which allows you to focus on other facets of your business so you can grow it bigger! You're a business owner, you deserve to be thinking of the bigger picture rather than being bogged down by the daily details that will lead up to that bigger picture.

Chapter 5: The Facebook Ads Manager

We have talked a lot about using Facebook ads, but you may not know where to start. Or, you're already using them, and you want to have a primer on your ads manager before your ads are run. In this chapter you'll be educated on everything you need to know when it comes to using Facebook Ads Manager.

Setting Up a Facebook Ads Manager Account

Before you can begin to advertise on Facebook, you'll have to set up the Ad's Manager account. First, you need to log into your Facebook and choose the drop-down menu that is found on the upper right-hand side of your page so that you can choose the create ads option. Ads Manager will create an account for you from there, and then send you through the steps you need to follow in order to run your first campaign.

Another option is for you to close out this screen by choosing the close button found on the lower left-hand side. Now you can click on the main menu at the top left-hand side so that you can reveal, and move through the various tools you'll have access to.

Explore Your Main Menu.

1. Now that you have opened up your main menu, you can see all of the options that you have access to (which will be explained below). After you get used to using Ads Manager, you'll see a new section that is titled, "frequently used." This is where all of the tools that you commonly use will be listed, so you don't have to go through and search for your beloved tools.

    a. Frequently used: You know what this section is, and we just touched on it above. However, if there is a tool that you use a lot, but is not listed here, click on the, "all tools" button at the bottom of your screen so you can see all of your tools.

b. Plan: This section is going to hold every tool you need to use in order to learn about the various aspects of your audience. This will enable you to come up with creative ideas for your ads.

    i. Audience insights: With this tool, you'll learn about the various audiences that are on Facebook. For example, you're wanting to figure out some advertising ideas, therefore, you're going to ask Facebook for the data as to who is connected to your page. Once you do this, you'll see a couple of different tabs that hold all of the information about those that are on your business page.

The first choice is your demographics page. This is going to show you the gender and age ranges of all the people that like your page. Depending on the dominant gender or age for your page, you may want to run ads that are aimed more towards them. You can even break your demographic down so that you can see how educated your member base is, what they do for a living, and their relationship status.

Now, when you move on to click the page likes tab, you can see more information that is going to help you in creating an ad that is targeted towards your demographic's interests. What you may not know is that inside of each ad campaign, you'll have the option to create separate ads that can target your audience based on the other pages that they like.

Click through all of the tabs and learn more about the clients that have liked your business page. You can likewise utilize this data so as to analyze your audience based on specific interests.

> ii. Creative hub: In the plan section there is a tool that is known as a creative hub, and it's a wonderful tool that allows you to create an ad mockup in order to share it with your team, as well as get fresh ideas.

2. Create and manage: In this section you'll find an assortment of tools that will be used when creating your ad, as well as managing your campaigns.

    c. Business manager: This tool was discussed above and allows you to create a team and delegate your tasks.

    d. Ads manager: Here you can run your campaigns as well as analyze the data from them. You're also going to be able to get customized reports, download the live data to be shared with your team, and even get Facebook pixel.

    e. Power editor: This is a strong advertising program that will give you the ability to create ad campaigns. This instrument will provide you with some more advanced options that can be used when starting any advertisement.

    f. Page posts: Here you'll be able to view all of the posts to your page and how people have been engaging with what you're posting. You'll have the ability to see the scheduled posts, the posts that have been published, and any ad posts. You'll also be able to view how each of your posts were received and the amount of people that viewed them. This tool should be used in order to check on your posts that have been published in order to see what is popular. That way, you can boost the post and get more engagement.

g. App ads helper: This program is helpful for any app developers to drive even more traffic to their ads.

h. Automated rules: Here you can define the parameters of your ad campaigns. You're going to find this tool extremely valuable since you'll have the ability to automate your alerts, and even take the actions necessary once certain parameters are met. So, if you need to take an ad down before it reaches $200 dollars, you're going to be able to. You're also going to see an estimated budget for each day based on the type of ad that you want to run.

3. Measure and report: You'll want to analyze how your ad is doing, which is why you'll use the measure and report section. In this section of your ad manager, you'll have the option of creating custom conversions in an effort to track how your advertisement is performing and if it's succeeding.

   i. Ads reporting: This tool will allow you to create a new ad for any ad that is being run or has run. In order to see an ad that you ran before, you'll be required to use the date selection tool so you can narrow your ads down to that specific ad. When you review your ads with ad reporting, you'll have the knowledge to create a better ad later on.

You'll find that this tool is especially helpful when you have to compare multiple campaigns in order to see how they are performing based on the primary performance metrics that are vital to you.

   j. Custom conversions: Even though Facebook Pixel is going to automatically track the standard actions that people perform when visiting your website, Facebook Pixel offers a customer conversion that is going to track the specific action that you want. For every ad account, you're going to be able to create up to 40 custom conversions at one time. Whenever you hit the maximum, delete what you're no longer using and move on to creating new ones. In order to create new ones, you'll click on, "create a new custom conversion" and then fill out the necessary information. Make sure that you're selecting a specific URL in order to effectively track conversions.

Tip: Once you have created a custom conversion, you'll need to refresh your page so that Pixel can fire up and allow Facebook to know that there is a custom conversion active.

k. Analytics: The analytics tool will help you in analyzing any data from Facebook Pixel, as well as your pages.

After you have begun to create ads and are fluently working with Pixel, this tool will be invaluable.

4. Assets: in this section, you'll have the ability to quickly and easily access any key assets that have been used in building your ads which includes your audiences that have been saved when you do ad targeting or any images that have been used before.

   a. Audiences: While you're always able to choose an audience when you create an ad, this tool will allow you to create an audience you can use later on.

Facebook allows you to create 3 different types of audiences. Custom audiences, lookalike audiences, and saved audiences. The audience type you choose is going to be based on the objective of your ad. Once you have selected your type of audience, Facebook is going to guide you through your different options.

   b. Images: Whenever you click on the image option, there is going to be a section of images that you previously used in your recent ads, or in boosted posts.

c. Pixels: Pixel is a vital asset for you when you're using a social media marketer. By clicking on the Pixel option, you can either install the Pixel or you can see data points that show where the Pixel fires on every page you have it installed . You'll be able to analyze the Pixel data so that you can create targeted ads.

d. Offline events: There will be important events you need to pay attention to off of Facebook. So, with offline events, you'll have a tool that is going to track those that see the ads about offline events so that you're able to feel more confident about these ads. Even though you're going to be able to track every conversion (and you're going to find that it's difficult to do this), you'll be able to create a more effective ad so that your campaign can be effective.

e. Product catalogs: This is going to be the perfect tool for any business that has an ecommerce website. Ultimately, you're going to see details from potential customers from your catalog depending on what interactions have been completed with your company. These catalog features can be utilized so as to make a product catalog through Facebook prompts. Once you have your catalog up, you're going to realize that it's a powerful diagnostic tool that is going to help you to be more effective when marketing your products.

f. Videos: The video option is going to allow you to see any video posted on your page. This is also going to be a helpful tool when uploading or managing videos.

5. Settings: Finally, this is where all of the information for your account will be stored and where you can update any information that you need to update.

Understanding the Tabs

Whenever you click on the ad manager option, you'll be opening up the Ad Manager tool. In this interface you'll see four different tabs that will hold an assortment of data to support you when evaluating ads.

1. Account overview: Here you're going to be able to glance at all of the ads you currently have out on Facebook. You're also going to be allowed to filter through your campaigns depending on if they are active or not.

2. Campaigns, ads tabs, ad sets: Before you can run an ad, you have to set aside the effort to make sense of what should be run and how well you think it's going to be run. What is going to be the click rate for your ad based on passed click rates? What is going to be your

cost per conversion? All of these will be metrics you need to know in order to be successful.

You'll be able to analyze all of your ads in this tab. Click on the tab that shows the groupings, and click on the group you want to analyze before you move on to use the performance breakdown columns. When you click on the performance column, you're going to notice that there are a few different options that you can use when it comes to viewing specific aspects of your campaign. All that has to be done is for you to choose the option you need to find, so as to see the related measurements.

There is additional data that you can examine in the breakdown segment where you can view exactly which day the conversions happened, or what device people were on when they clicked on your ad. You'll have the option to customize these columns so that you can create unique reports that can be shared with your team, or examine so that you can discover what is pushing you closer to success. In order to save these customized reports, click on the save report button and provide your report with a name.

Creating a Facebook Ad with Ads Manager

Any time that you go to create a campaign, your ad will need to move through 3 steps.

1. Select the, "create ad" button which is located at the top right of your ads manager so you can begin to make an advertisement. This is going to open up the campaign level so you're able to choose the objective of your ad.

2. From here you'll move on to the, "ad set stage" which is going to allow you to effectively define who is in your audience. You may also use the audience tool that was mentioned earlier. If you have already saved an audience, you'll choose that audience here.

3. The last step in this process is to create your ad. Whenever you click on the Facebook page or even Instagram account, you'll then choose how you need your promotion to be shown. Once you have done that, you're going to review your ad, and place your order so that your campaign can get started.

In the end, Facebook Ads Manager will be the best place for you to create all of your ad campaigns. The analytics that you're able to access in the Ad Manager is going to enable you to tailor your ads to meet your specific business needs. However, having a vast targeted audience is going to help you to keep the costs of your ads low.

Chapter 6: Facebook Ad Campaigns

First things first, you need to decide how Facebook advertisements will fit into your marketing schedule. This is going to assist you with saving cash and keeping you from flying by the seat of your pants with no clear path, and ultimately, no success.

In order to see consistent results, you must first figure out where your sales will be funneling from, which is going to enable you to manipulate your Facebook ads. So, let's start by answering these four questions to help you when it comes to defining your strategy.

1. Are you able to create unique content for your business?

2. What is your end goal? Are you trying to get new leads for your business, or are you trying to get more subscribers?

3. Are you working with an email list? How many people are on your email list? How many of those people are actively interacting with you through your emails?

4. Do you have any consistent web traffic to work with?

After you have sat down and answered those four questions, you're ready to move on and examine the 3 best promoting methodologies that you can used based on how you answered the questions above.

1. Provide content that is both free and warm to your audience. The whole point of content marketing is to set your business apart from others. Ensure that you provide your audience with free content that will entertain, inspire, or educate your customers. You'll have the option of using videos, blog posts, or lead magnets.

2. Engage those on your email list. When you deliver your ad, not only on Facebook, but also through email, it's going to be more effective than just using one method. Customers will see your ad in their inbox and then it's going to catch their attention when they are scrolling through Facebook.

3. Retarget your website visitors. In the event that you have installed Facebook Pixel on your business site, Pixel can provide you with the

option of targeting people who have recently clicked on your website. However, a retargeting strategy will be the second phase of your content first strategy. You'll build a custom audience of those who have engaged with any of the content that has been posted on your page. After you've completed that step, you'll run a direct response campaign specific to those people when you're promoting your business.

Picking a Campaign Objective Based on What Your Goal Is

Facebook campaigns are structured to have 3 levels. The first is your campaign, then your ad set, and finally your ad. But everything else is going to be dependent on how you set up your campaign objective.

At the campaign level, you'll choose what your objective is when it comes to what action you want people to take whenever they see your ad. There are three different categories that you can browse; conversion, awareness, consideration.

The goal that you decide to use depends on the strategy you intended to use. If you decide to utilize a substance first methodology, your most logical option might be to utilize a video so as to get video views. Presently, should you find that you're needing to run a retargeting effort so as to push individuals towards your site, you'll pick transformations or traffic. It's prescribed that you work in reverse from your objective so as to make sense of what your goal is.

Building Your Ideal Audience

Since you have picked your battle structure, you're going to need to focus on your group of spectators with the goal that you can make your advertisement effective. There are 3 unique ways that you can characterize your group of spectators.

1. Target demographics and interests. This will be the least demanding route for you to target new individuals who have never cooperated with your business. You should choose what

your statistic imperatives will be. With regards to the nitty gritty focusing on segment, you'll limit your crowd by picking between socio economics, interests, and practices.

Facebook makes it to where you don't have to decide how big your objective client base is going to be. You'll discover that you'll receive better results when you use a layered approach. You'll almost certainly pick a blend of interests and practices so as to zero in on who your optimal client would be.

Your next move is to narrow down your audience by using an "and" condition. You'll click, "narrow audience" and then choose the life event that people are currently going through.

2. Target your custom audience with people who already know about your business. You can target individuals who have cooperated with your business here and there before, whether it be through Facebook, your email advertising, or your website. A custom group of clients can help you in conveying the absolute best outcomes with regards to retargeting efforts since you're going to, as of

now, be hitting on a crowd of people that is heated up and knows your identity and, in all likelihood, prefers you. When it comes to creating a custom audience, you're going to have 4 categories to choose from.

q. Customer files will be your email customers. You'll upload or import your data into Facebook so it's able to cross match the people on your list to their profile on Facebook. This custom audience is going to be a complete game changer in the event that you have an existing subscriber list, since you'll be targeting that audience specifically with your ad campaigns.

r. Website Custom crowd will be made from the action on your site. You'll have the alternative to utilize Facebook Pixel and then change "following" to follow those that go to your site. This crowd will be ideal for retargeting. Inside this focused-on group of spectators, you can make distinctive site custom crowds dependent on what pages they visited, to what extent they stayed, and what moves they made on your site.

s. App activity will enable you to include people who have completed a specific action on your application. This is similar to the custom audience for your website, but it will be different because the action happens in an app rather than on a website.

t. Engagement audiences will include anyone that has interacted with something that you posted on your Facebook. Right now, you're able to choose between four types of engagement such as video, lead ad, page, and canvas.

> i. Video engagement allows you to group people together based on how much of your video they have watched. This is one of the fastest ways to retarget your audience.

- ii. Canvas and lead ad will target anyone who has ever interacted with one of your advertisements.

- iii. Page engagement is going to target those that have interacted with your Facebook page.

It's important for you to keep in mind that every custom clientele group will have different match rates. This is something that you're going to need to take into account when you're planning what sort of commitment group of spectators you need to target.

3. Target lookalike audiences. Lookalike audiences are considered to be the holy grail of ad targeting on Facebook, since they deliver consistently good results. In other words, lookalike audiences are effective because Facebook uses an algorithm in order to create them. These audiences are created by Facebook taking data points from a source audience that has been preselected so that similar people can be found. In the end, it's going to be similar to cloning an audience that already exists.

Building and Testing Your Ad Creative

The very last part of your campaign structure is the ad level, which is also known as your "creative." Your ad is going to be what is placed on Facebook for others to see. Here, you choose your ad format and any creativity that you're placing in it, such as your videos, images, URLS so on and so forth. What your Facebook ad looks like is going to depend on the advertising strategy that you picked earlier. A couple of goals will compel what advertisement designs you can utilize.

The best practice for Facebook ad creative is to use multiple ads while running your campaigns. You should not stop after you have created one ad. Instead, use different ads with different images or videos.

Always make sure that you're introducing new ads when your relevancy score begins to drop. The score is going to drop whenever people continue to see the same ad over and over again, which is why you should try to create new ads to ensure that you don't drive away potential customers by using the same ad that they have seen a million times before.

When you're running a retargeting campaign, you'll need to use a single image advertisement since it's the most common ad format. Whenever your score starts to decrease, you will have several different paths that you can follow.

1. Split test the ads format: Here is where you'll be introducing a new ad with a different format.

2. Split test the image: Choose another single image ad but use a different picture.

3. Split test the copy: Duplicate your ad but change the copy to ensure that it's not a replica of the original ad.

One of the most common mistakes that's made is to kill a campaign in order to start a new one. In the event that your first ad doesn't give you the results that you want, don't kill it, add in new ads instead.

In the end, before you start to create Facebook campaigns, make sure you're taking the time to figure out what your strategy is and where your sales funnel is, to ensure that you're pushing your business towards success.

Chapter 7: Using the Facebook Events Manager

Before you have the option of setting up the Pixel event you'll need to enter a Pixel event code on each of your web pages. However, Facebook has streamlined how the Pixel events are set up thanks to the Facebook Event Setup Tool for web. This tool is going to enable you to set up events without having to enter a code. Keep in mind that you'll have to install the base Pixel code if you have not already.

The new cordless setup is going to allow you to add in certain actions such as URL clicks, page load triggers or button likes to your website.

Installing Facebook Pixel Events

Facebook Pixel can be a great tool when it comes to pushing data from your website to Facebook. The information that is collected will assist you in learning more about your customers and how they are interacting with your website, so you're able to improve ad sequences. There are two parts of Facebook Pixel that you need to understand before using it.

1. Your Facebook primary code is a unique ID for your specific Facebook Pixel and what account it's linked to. This will allow you to track whenever a specific page is going to be seen. Once you have set up this part of your Pixel, your Facebook will begin to collect data from your website.

2. The second part of the Pixel will enable you to track certain actions taken by your customers on your website. These insights will show you how often a customer moves through your website, which is going to create funnels and ads based on the actions that they take.

You're going to have the option of adding the base code to your site manually or you can have an event partner set up the code. Depending on the platform and the settings tied to it, you may have your event code set up as well. Once Pixel base has been installed, you'll use the event setup tool so as to add occasions to your website. You can access these tools by opening up your ad managers and choosing Pixels under your event manager.

Once you find the Facebook Pixel page under events manager, you'll need to pick your Pixel, and then select settings. Under event setup, you'll click on, "go to event setup tool." Since you have completed this step, you should enter the URL where you're wanting to install the Pixel event before moving on to click on the button that says, "open website." This should open a pop-up window that will prompt you to choose the event you would like to be measured. The trigger for this event is going to be the customer going to that page and allowing it to fully load on their device.

When you're attempting to install an event on your page, you should click on "track new button," or "track a URL."

1. Tracking an event through a URL is going to take you to a drop-down menu where you'll pick what event you're wanting to track.

2. Tracking an event with a button click will be an event triggered by a specific action such as a button click. Facebook is going to open your

website and highlight each clickable button. You should choose the button that you need to use while setting up your event. After you have chosen the button, you'll confirm the event. After completing this step, you'll see it appear on the Facebook Event Setup.

3. Review your Pixel events. After you have added each event that you want to track you'll finish your set up, and then confirm your actions by clicking on finish. You should see a window that says that your event set up has been completed and you're going to given the option to check out your Pixel events to make sure that they are set up properly.

Testing the Firing of Your Pixel Events

After setting up a Pixel event, it's time to test it to ensure that information is getting read properly. There are two different tools that you can use in order to help you with this step.

1. Facebook Pixel helper is an extension of chrome that is going to enable you to read

Pixels that come from your site or other sites. This is a helpful tool because it can scan each site that you visit and provide you with a summary of Pixels available for that site. Once you install the extension, you'll need to navigate to a page where you have installed the event code. From here you'll click on the Pixel helper icon that is located on the chrome toolbar. You're going to be able to see information about any event that you're tracking for that page.

2. Also, on the Pixel page you can select the diagnostic tab so you can see all of the detailed insights about how your Pixel is firing. You'll be able to see recommendations for updates or any information that your Pixel could be missing. In the event that everything is set up right, the information will be able to be passed between Facebook and your website. However, if you see errors or warnings about your Pixel, you'll need to troubleshoot it.

Creating Custom Audiences From Facebook Pixel Event Data

After your Pixel events have been set up, what are you going to be able to do with this data? Well for one, you can create a custom audience from your website visitors in order to deliver messages based on how they react to your content. When it comes to creating this custom audience, you'll open up ad manager and navigate to audiences. From there, you're going to create an audience with the new menu that drops down.

Now, in the new window that appears, you'll choose the option, "website traffic." Another window is going to appear and you're going to see a variety of options that will allow you to refine your audience.

If you want to add in everyone who has ever visited your site, but has not made any purchases, you'll need to add in exclusion criteria. Make sure that you remember that all your custom audiences will be dynamic. They will always be populated with new website visitors who are fulfilling the criteria that you have set up. Just make sure you also remember that it's going to take up to 24 hours for the update to show the latest results.

Combining Pixel Event Data With Facebook Product Catalog in Order to Improve Ads

If you're selling online, you're going to have the option of creating a product catalog that showcases your assets. Pixel can be attached to this, in order to better track the ad options whenever you have to perform follow ups or any cross selling.

To start a Facebook catalog, you'll open your ad manager and then choose catalog under assets. Next you're going to create catalog and choose your industry. When the catalog window pops up, you'll pick how to populate your catalog. If you want to, you can upload products yourself by uploading the product information.

Should you want to import your products, you can load them from the eCommerce platform such as WooCommerce, Shopify, and so many more. Each platform will be programed to know how to format and deliver the information to Facebook for the product catalog. Now you'll choose your business as it appears on your drop-down menu before naming your catalog. If you decided to use an eCommerce platform, you'll need to finish setup and follow all the prompts on your screen.

1. Upload products by opening up a new catalog. Click on the product data source before adding products. You'll need to pick from the following options to add items to your catalog.

    u. Connect Facebook Pixels to your website so you can ensure your catalog remains updated. You'll have the option to add specific code about every product to your Pixels. This process is complex and will use the manual option.

    v. Add manually by filling out every product that needs to be inserted into your catalog.

    w. Using data feeds will upload CSV data feed files that contain your product information.

2. Connect Facebook Pixel to your catalog. Once your catalog has been created, you'll connect Pixel to it so that you can collect more data on how website visitors are interacting with the products you place online. In order to connect your Pixel you'll open up your catalog and click on events data sources tab before clicking on the Pixel, and then click on done. When you connect your Pixel, you'll unlock 2 ad types that will do better for your online sales and will provide you with more accurate reporting.

   1. Conversion ads will optimize your ad delivery in order to deliver the ad to the people in your audience who are most likely going to perform a specific type of conversion behavior. These ads will allow you to see a direct cost per conversion which will make reporting and forecasting ROI that much more accurate.

Whenever your campaign gets set up, you can choose the website option in the conversion section and pick the Pixel and conversion event. Conversion ads have to have at least 50 conversions in 7 days in order to be fully optimized. If it doesn't, the ad delivery is going to be too slow or not as effective until Facebook is able to collect the information that is coming from your Pixel.

> 2. Dynamic product ads will work if your product catalog and Pixel are connected. This ad type is the best way to follow up, cross sell, or upset, and it can also boost sales and conversion rates. Dynamic product ads will be triggered by a customer's action your website. Based on what data has been collected by Pixel, Facebook will help you in identifying what product or product category people are interacting with. The ad will show the product that they viewed or even products that are similar.

Take for example, your customer browses the shoes on your store but doesn't buy anything. You'll have the option to trigger an ad that is going to show the shoe or a range of different products. Or, if they add the shoe to their cart but don't buy it, encourage them to buy with a coupon code.

In order to create a dynamic product ad you'll choose the catalog sales for your campaign objective. Then you'll choose the product catalog that is tied to that campaign. Once you get to the ad level, you'll pick what you want your customers to see. If you're wanting to show a group of products or specific products, you'll click on the add button before filtering the products to what needs to be shown in your ad.

Below that you'll need to pick your triggers which will be the dynamic products that the ad will show. For Ad Creative, you'll choose the type of ad you want to be displayed on Facebook. If you're not wanting Facebook to populate the information, you'll have the option to customize the images and text.

Analyzing Your Pixel Data

The Pixel page in your events manager is going to display all of the Pixel data. You'll select the "data source" heading, which will allow you to examine an overview of all the data that has been inputted, along with details from any partner integrations mixed in with all of the custom conversions that have been created.

The overview of your Pixel will display the most recent 30 days of information so that if you're running a report for specific dates, you can find it. It's recommended that you report the data at the same time every month so that the information is accurate. When you create a custom audience, the Pixel will be able to go back 180 days and help you use that to create a custom audience.

Chapter 8: Facebook Pixel

So, what is Facebook Pixel? A lot of people tend to forget about Facebook Pixel because the internet is filled with cookies. Cookies will track the movements of your website visitors. In the end, Pixels are just the same as cookies.

Facebook Pixel Functions

Pixels have multiple actions that will aid you while you're creating your marketing campaigns.

1. Track conversions: Conversions will be any action that your visitors complete. Facebook Pixel is able to keep track of 9 different types of conversions that will be available to you in order for you to improve your conversion rate and targeting. Take for example, you're running a campaign that costs $1 per click and get up to 500 clicks. Pixel is going to be able to tell you exactly how many people clicked on the ad and how it's actually converted.

2. Optimize ads for conversions: One of the biggest differences between Google Analytics and Facebook Pixel will be how Facebook uses the information collected by Pixel. Instead of just showing you what is seen, Facebook will collect the data and then target people who are similar to those that are already being converted. Therefore, by optimizing your targeting which will help to improve your chances for success.

3. Retargeting ads: Online, retargeting will be when you send ads to those that have already shown an interest in your site or have interacted with you before. Facebook's Pixels will allow you to retarget people who have performed a specific action on your website.

Take for instance, if you visit an airline website to search for trips, you'll notice that once you leave the site, there will be more ads that are related to traveling. You're not imagining this. You're being targeted so they can get you to spend money on their site.

Most marketers know that retargeting customers will be easier to convert because they have already visited your site. That means that they are more likely to become a normal customer.

Creating a Facebook Pixel

Facebook Pixel can sound scary, but it's a lot easier to do than you think. Here we will go through the steps to creating a Facebook Pixel.

1. Enter your ad account and select the menu choice. From this point you should go to "all tools" which is going to expand the menu. You'll then click on "Pixel" which can be found under measure and report.

2. Facebook will then prompt you to create your own Pixel.

3. The only thing that you're going to need to do is provide a name for your Pixel. The name is not going to be public therefore you can name it something that is logical to you.

4. You'll be required to accept the terms of conditions.

5. Now you'll click on the option that will give you a new menu. When adding Pixel to your website, a lot of people decide to manually install it, or you can email the instructions to a developer if that is easier for you.

6. Last, you'll copy the code that is provided and add it to your website.

Note: When using Shopify, you may find that you prefer to use method 4 (which can be found in the next section) when it comes to adding Pixel to your site. If this is the case, you'll want to use the integration or tag manager option rather than manually install the code yourself one.

From there you're going to click on the Shopify icon and then copy the integration code that is provided.

Adding Pixel to WordPress or Shopify

There are a couple of different methods that can be used in order to add Pixel to your website.

1. Direct upload to WordPress. Follow these simple steps in order to install Pixel.

x. Go to your WordPress dashboard and click on the left menu. From there you'll click on appearance and editor.

y. file. On the right-hand side you'll move to theme files, you'll scroll down till you see the theme header or header.php. You're now going to be able to edit your WordPress theme's header

z. Scroll down until you can see the closing head tag.

aa. Add in a few blank lines between the closing head tag and any code before it. Now you'll insert the Pixel code to the new blank lines.

bb. Save your file and upload it with an FTP program.

Note: When you decide to change your theme, you'll have to go through this process again because Pixel will be removed from the theme changes.

2. Through a WordPress plugin. This is recommended when you're inserting headers

and footers. But there are a variety of plugins that you can use if you want.

cc. From the left menu, choose plugins and add new.

dd. Use your search on the lower right side in order to find the plugin you want to use.

ee. Install and activate the header and footer plugin to your website.

ff. Now move back to your menu and choose settings before clicking on insert headers and footers.

gg. open your plugin and search for scripts in header before pasting the Pixel code in the proper box.

hh. Save and refresh your page.

One of the best benefits when it comes to this plugin is that when you change themes, your Pixel is still going to be on your website.

Note: If you're using Pixel on one website, you can install the Facebook Pixel helper which is located on Chrome. This is going to allow you to see any events that are happening in real time.

3. Shopify direct upload. This method should only be utilized if you feel comfortable updating your site's theme.

    ii. Got Shopify and click on the online store.

    jj. On your new menu you'll click on themes.

    kk. In the themes section you'll click on actions and then click on edit code.

    ll. Under the layout folder you'll need to click on the theme that you're currently using.

    mm. Scroll down until you see the closing head tag.

    nn. Make sure you add in a few lines before the head tag and any code that comes before it. You'll then enter your Pixel code into these blank lines.

oo. Click save.

4. Shopify integration. Since some people are not comfortable when it comes to editing code, Shopify has created a simpler method so you don't have to mess with any of the code.

   pp. Go to Shopify and click on the online store off the left-hand side menu.

   qq. In your new menu, select preferences.

   rr. ON this new page, move down until you see a box that asks you about your Pixel id.

   ss. Paste your Pixel id into the box.

   tt. Save your new changes.

Installing and using Pixel may end up being the most effective marketing strategy that you'll decide to use. It's only going to be a few steps that you have to follow in order to have access to powerful analytics on your website.

Chapter 9: Reasons Why You Should Use Facebook Advertising

You have seen how you can use Facebook for your business, now let's look at the reasons why you should use Facebook for advertising.

1. Facebook advertising is extremely effective. Because of how many people are on Facebook, it's hard to ignore that Facebook is a major part of everyone's life. In fact, Facebook is considered to be one of the top advertising channels online because digital ads make up 51% of total advertising in the United States.

2. Simple set up and fast results. Setting up a Facebook campaign is going to take very little time and will provide you with excellent results. Digital advertising produces terrific ROI and will be extremely fast when you assign the best campaign strategy with the best product that you have to offer. Facebook has the tools to help you drive traffic to your

website and even allows you to boost single posts.

3. You can reach the perfect audience. You have already seen how you can design the perfect clientele that will help you when it comes to targeting the right demographic. It's also going to make your advertising more successful.

4. Facebook campaigns are customizable. You'll be able to create the perfect ad experience because it will only be seen by your specified audience choice. All of this is made possible because of the different ad formats that Facebook provides you when you create your ad campaigns.

5. Facebook adds new features every month. Because of how adaptive Facebook is your ads will constantly evolve to reach the perfect audience.

6. You can set your own budget on Facebook which is going to allow you to advertise for as little as $1. Even though this is a small budget, your campaign is still going to reach a lot of people.

7. You can easily track your performance and ROI with the analytic tools that Facebook provides such as your ad manager.

8. You'll get an edge over your competitors because not everyone is using Facebook, or they are not using it properly. therefore, you're going to gain an advantage over your competition. So, exploit it while you can!

9. Facebook is compelling with regards to push going back and forth leads down the pipeline. This strategy will work for any marketer that is trying to target their clients that have already visited your website which means that they are most likely going to be attracted to your business on some level.

10. Facebook makes it easy for you to find new leads. As you saw earlier, you'll have the tools with Facebook business manager that will let you look at people who are interested in specific hobbies or certain pages that will lead you to more people who could be interested in your business but have yet to hear about you.

Conclusion

In this book, you were able to see how to build your Facebook business, and the variety of tools that Facebook has to offer you when it comes to growing your business.

Now that you have read this book, you should know how to create a business page, business group, and even Facebook Event Manger.

There is so much more that will be there for you to utilize in an effort to grow your business, but you'll want to start out small and grow your business that way. Regardless of whether you're an entrepreneur or a billionaire, you're going to have the potential to grow into a multimillion-dollar company. But it's not going to happen overnight, which is why you need to start managing your business as best as you can now.

Do not overlook how much Facebook is able to be able to help you!

Thank you for downloading this book and please remember to leave a review!

Works Cited

5 Reasons You Should Be Advertising on Facebook. (n.d.). Retrieved from https://www.wordstream.com/blog/ws/2015/10/14/advertising-on-facebook

5 Reasons Your Business Must Use Facebook Advertising. (n.d.). Retrieved from https://www.koozai.com/blog/social-media/facebook-social-media/benefits-of-facebook-advertising/

Cannon, T. (2019, January 16). How to Use Facebook Ads Manager: A Guide for Beginners. Retrieved from https://www.socialmediaexaminer.com/facebook-ads-manager-guide-for-beginners/

Chieruzzi, M. (n.d.). TOP 5 Reasons to Advertise on Facebook. Retrieved from https://adespresso.com/guides/facebook-ads-beginner/why-you-should-advertise-on-facebook-now/

Dara. (2018, April 16). How to Get Verified on Facebook: A Step-by-Step Guide. Retrieved from https://blog.hootsuite.com/how-to-get-verified-on-facebook/

Facebook Pixel 101: A Practical Guide for Facebook Ad Novice. (2018, December 12). Retrieved from https://tredigital.com/facebook_pixel/

Fraser, L. (2019, April 30). How to Use the Facebook Event Setup Tool. Retrieved from https://www.socialmediaexaminer.com/how-to-use-facebook-event-setup-tool/

How to Create an Engaging Facebook Group for Your Business. (2018, December 11). Retrieved from https://mavsocial.com/create-a-facebook-group-for-your-business/

Lawrance, C. (2019, January 16). How to Set Up an Effective Facebook Ad Campaign. Retrieved from https://www.socialmediaexaminer.com/how-to-set-up-an-effective-facebook-ad-campaign/

Newberry, C., & Dara. (2018, July 27). How to Create a Facebook Business Page in 8 Simple Steps. Retrieved from https://blog.hootsuite.com/steps-to-create-a-facebook-business-page/

Pinkman, K. (2017, December 07). A Step-By-Step Guide to Using Facebook Business Manager. Retrieved from https://www.ecwid.com/blog/how-to-use-facebook-business-manager.html

Urrutia, K. (2018, February 25). How to Use Facebook Ads Effectively. Retrieved from https://voymedia.com/how-to-use-facebook-ads-effectively/

www.ingramcontent.com/pod-product-compliance
Lightning Source LLC
Chambersburg PA
CBHW020557220526
45463CB00006B/2342